THE COGNITIVE EFFECTS OF ARTIFICIAL INTELLIGENCE OVER-RELIANCE ON HUMAN PHYSIOLOGY AND MENTAL HEALTH

THE COGNITIVE EFFECTS OF ARTIFICIAL INTELLIGENCE OVER-RELIANCE ON HUMAN PHYSIOLOGY AND MENTAL HEALTH

DAKOTA FRANDSEN

First Printing, 2025

CONTENTS

This research essay synthesizes current scientific literature on the cognitive effects of AI over-reliance, presenting evidence-based strategies for maintaining human cognitive health while maximizing the benefits of human-AI collaboration.

Abstract

The rapid integration of artificial intelligence (AI) systems into daily human activities has fundamentally altered cognitive processes, decision-making patterns, and neural pathways. This research essay examines the physiological and psychological consequences of AI over-reliance, with particular emphasis on negative cognitive effects including attention degradation, memory impairment, and reduced critical thinking capacity. Through analysis of contemporary neuroscience research and behavioral studies, this paper identifies evidence-based strategies for maintaining cognitive autonomy while leveraging AI capabilities for mutual benefit. The findings suggest that balanced human-AI interaction requires deliberate cognitive exercise, maintained autonomy in decision-making, and structured digital detox protocols to preserve essential human cognitive functions.

Introduction

The 21st century has seen an unprecedented shift in human-technology interaction due to the widespread adoption of artificial intelligence (AI) systems. From smartphone assistants to advanced decision-support tools, AI is now integral to cognitive tasks once exclusively performed by humans. While these technologies offer remarkable benefits in productivity and problem-solving, emerging research highlights concerning patterns of cognitive dependency that could fundamentally alter human neuroplasticity and mental health.

The concept of "cognitive offloading"—using external tools to reduce mental effort—is not new.

However, modern AI systems' scope and sophistication pose unique challenges to human cognitive development and maintenance. Unlike traditional tools that enhance specific abilities, AI can perform complex reasoning, pattern recognition, and decision-making that closely mimic human cognitive processes. This similarity raises the risk of cognitive atrophy through disuse, much like muscle weakness from physical inactivity.

Growing evidence from neuroscience and cognitive psychology suggests that excessive reliance on AI systems can induce significant and measurable changes in the human brain. These alterations include shifts in neural connectivity, diminished attention spans, and impaired executive function. Such changes have profound implications for individual cognitive health, societal resilience, and human autonomy in an increasingly automated world. This essay will examine the scientific evidence of AI over-reliance's cognitive effects, explore the underlying neurobiological mechanisms, and propose evidence-based strategies for preserving cognitive health while maximizing the advantages of human-AI collaboration. The goal is not to advocate for AI avoidance but to establish frameworks for sustainable and mutually beneficial human-AI interaction that safeguards essential human cognitive capacities.

Neurobiological Underpinnings of AI Over-Reliance

2.1 NEUROPLASTICITY AND USE-DEPENDENT BRAIN CHANGES

The brain's remarkable capacity for neuroplasticity—its ability to reorganize neural pathways based on experience—is crucial for understanding how AI over-reliance affects cognitive function. Research, including that by Merzenich et al. (2014), demonstrates a "use it or lose it" principle:

frequently activated neural pathways strengthen, while unused connections weaken or disappear. When individuals consistently delegate tasks like navigation, calculation, memory retrieval, or decision-making to AI, the corresponding neural networks experience reduced activation.

Neuroimaging studies, employing functional magnetic resonance imaging (fMRI), have revealed decreased activity in the hippocampus, prefrontal cortex, and anterior cingulate cortex in heavy technology users compared to control groups (Ward et al., 2017; Loh & Kanai, 2016). The hippocampus, vital for spatial navigation and episodic memory, shows particularly pronounced changes in individuals heavily dependent on GPS systems. A landmark study by Bohbot et al. (2017) found that habitual GPS users had significantly less gray matter in the hippocampus and exhibited impaired spatial memory compared to those who regularly used traditional navigation methods. These findings suggest that offloading cognitive tasks to AI can lead to measurable structural brain changes within relatively short periods.

2.2 ATTENTION NETWORKS AND COGNITIVE CONTROL

The human attention system comprises three distinct networks: alerting, orienting, and executive attention (Posner & Petersen, 1990). AI over-reliance primarily impacts the executive attention network, which is responsible for resolving cognitive conflict, maintaining focus, and allocating attention. Rosen et al. (2013) demonstrated that individuals who frequently multitask with digital devices exhibit reduced capacity for sustained attention and increased distractibility.

The constant availability of AI assistance fosters "continuous partial attention"—a state where individuals maintain superficial awareness of multiple information streams without developing deep focus on any single task (Stone, 2006). This cognitive pattern is linked to increased cortisol production, reduced working memory capacity, and impaired learning consolidation (Ophir et al., 2009). Neurotransmitter systems also adapt to AI usage patterns. The dopamine reward system, which drives learning and exploration, becomes dysregulated when AI provides immediate answers and solutions. This can lead to reduced intrinsic motivation for problem-solving and decreased tolerance for uncertainty or ambiguity—cognitive states essential for creativity and innovation (Schultz, 2015).

Cognitive Consequences of AI Over-Reliance

3.1 MEMORY IMPAIRMENT AND EXTERNAL MEMORY DEPENDENCE

One of the most documented effects of AI over-reliance is "digital amnesia" or the "Google effect" (Sparrow et al., 2011)—the tendency to forget information believed to be readily accessible digitally. While seemingly efficient, research suggests significant costs. Barr et al. (2015) conducted longitudinal studies showing that individuals consistently using AI for information retrieval exhibited decreased activation in memory consolidation networks and reduced performance on recall tasks. The transactive memory system—our ability to remember where information is stored rather than the information itself—becomes overly dependent on digital sources, creating vulnerability when those sources are unavailable.

More concerning is the impact on episodic memory formation. Ward et al. (2017) found that the mere presence of a smartphone, even when turned off, reduces cognitive capacity and working memory performance. This implies that the potential for AI assistance alone creates cognitive changes that persist beyond active use. The implications extend to learning and skill acquisition. Mueller & Oppenheimer (2014) demonstrated that students who take notes by hand show better comprehension and retention than those using digital devices, even with AI-assisted features like autocorrect. This suggests that the cognitive effort required for manual processing contributes to learning in ways AI assistance cannot replace.

3.2 ATTENTION DEGRADATION AND FOCUS DISORDERS

AI systems are designed to capture and maintain user attention through sophisticated engagement algorithms. This creates an environment of constant cognitive stimulation that can lead to attention disorders resembling ADHD symptoms, even in individuals without underlying neurological conditions (Rosen et al., 2013). "Attention residue" occurs when individuals rapidly switch between AI-assisted tasks, leaving cognitive resources tied up in previous activities (Sophie Leroy, 2009). This fragmentation of attention reduces overall cognitive efficiency and impairs the development of sustained focus capabilities.

Research by Mark et al. (2016) using experience sampling methods found that heavy AI users exhibited significantly reduced attention spans and increased difficulty with tasks requiring sustained concentration. Brain imaging studies revealed decreased gray matter density in areas associated with attention control, including the anterior cingulate cortex and lateral prefrontal cortex. The development of "cognitive impatience" is another significant concern. AI systems provide near-instantaneous responses, conditioning users to expect immediate gratification for cognitive effort. This creates difficulty tolerating the uncertainty and extended processing time required for complex problem-solving and creative thinking (Carr, 2010).

3.3 REDUCED CRITICAL THINKING AND DECISION-MAKING AUTONOMY

Perhaps the most concerning effect of AI overreliance is the degradation of critical thinking skills and autonomous decision-making capacity. When AI systems provide recommendations or solutions, users often accept these outputs without adequate evaluation, leading to "automation bias" (Parasuraman & Riley, 1997). Studies by Goddard et al. (2012) found that individuals regularly using AI decision-support systems showed decreased activation in brain regions associated with critical evaluation and skeptical thinking. This effect persists even when participants are explicitly instructed to critically evaluate AI recommendations.

The cognitive process of generating multiple solutions to problems—divergent thinking—also shows impairment with heavy AI use. Acar et al. (2017) demonstrated that individuals relying on AI for creative tasks showed reduced originality and flexibility in subsequent creative endeavors, even when AI was unavailable. Decision-making autonomy is further compromised by the development of learned helplessness when facing cognitive challenges. Individuals become conditioned to seek AI assistance rather than engaging their own problem-solving capabilities, leading to reduced confidence in their cognitive abilities and increased anxiety when AI systems are unavailable (Seligman, 1972; updated context by Maier & Seligman, 2016).

Physiological and Mental Health Consequences

4.1 STRESS RESPONSE AND CORTISOL DYSREGULATION

Over-reliance on AI systems significantly impacts human physiology and mental health, extending beyond cognitive alterations to affect stress response systems, sleep patterns, and social interactions.

Physiological Impacts

AI over-reliance dysregulates the hypothalamic-pituitary-adrenal (HPA) axis, which controls cortisol production. Constant AI connectivity creates chronic low-level stress as the brain anticipates interruptions and processes digital information (Thomée et al., 2011). Elevated cortisol levels are observed in heavy technology users, especially when devices are inaccessible (Rosen et al., 2014). This stress leads to sleep disturbances, immune system suppression, and increased anxiety and depression. Extreme manifestations include "phantom vibrations" and "nomophobia" (fear of being without a mobile phone), reflecting neurochemical changes in stress pathways that diminish quality of life (Clayton et al., 2011).

Sleep Disruption and Circadian Rhythm Disorders

AI systems, particularly those integrated with screen-based devices, disrupt sleep quality and circadian rhythms. Blue light from screens suppresses melatonin, and cognitive stimulation from AI interaction further impedes sleep (Chang et al., 2015). Individuals using AI-enabled devices before bedtime experience delayed sleep onset, reduced REM sleep, and impaired sleep consolidation (Gradisar et al., 2013). Cognitive arousal from AI, especially systems with unpredictable rewards like social media algorithms, induces hypervigilance that persists during sleep. Sleep fragmentation from AI notifications and compulsive checking leads to chronic sleep deprivation, creating a cycle where impaired cognitive function increases AI reliance, further disrupting sleep (Levenson et al., 2016).

Social Isolation and Interpersonal Skill Degradation

AI over-reliance contributes to social isolation and degradation of interpersonal skills. Increased comfort with AI interaction can lead to social anxiety and reduced empathy (Turkle, 2011). Heavy AI and social media use correlate with increased loneliness (Primack et al., 2017). Replacing human interaction with AI lacks the complex emotional and social feedback essential for maintaining interpersonal skills. Heavy AI users may develop "digital autism," characterized by difficulty reading social cues, impaired emotional recognition, reduced eye contact, and challenges with unstructured social interaction (Radesky et al., 2014).

EVIDENCE-BASED MITIGATION STRATEGIES

Cognitive Training and Mental Exercise Protocols

Interventions can counteract negative cognitive effects of AI over-reliance while preserving benefits of human-AI collaboration. Cognitive training programs strengthen attention, working memory, and executive function, reversing AI-related cognitive decline. The dual n-back task improves cognitive control and reduces dependency on external cognitive aids, showing significant improvements in fluid intelligence and sustained attention (Jaeggi et al., 2008; Au et al., 2015).

Mindfulness-based cognitive training also addresses AI over-reliance, with just four 20-minute sessions improving working memory capacity, executive attention, and cognitive flexibility. These improvements are linked to increased gray matter density in critical brain regions (Zeidan et al., 2010; Hölzel et al., 2011).

Deliberate practice without AI assistance maintains cognitive autonomy. Cognitive skills require regular, challenging practice to maintain peak performance (Ericsson & Pool, 2016). "Cognitive cross-training"—practicing tasks AI systems typically handle (e.g., mental arithmetic, spatial navigation)—maintains better cognitive performance and reduces dependency on external aids (Kelly & Garavan, 2005).

Digital Detox and Structured AI Abstinence

Periodic abstinence from AI systems, or "digital detox," is crucial for cognitive health. Short-term reductions in AI use (one week) improve well-being, life satisfaction, and cognitive performance (Brailovskaia et al., 2020). Attention restoration theory suggests AI-free periods allow cognitive systems to recover from constant stimulation (Kaplan, 1995).

Structured digital sabbaths (weekly 24-hour AI abstinence) improve attention span, reduce anxiety, and enhance sleep quality within four weeks, increasing connectivity in default mode networks, indicating cognitive rest and restoration (Turel et al., 2018).

Implementing "friction" in AI access (making AI slightly more difficult to use) reduces compulsive usage while maintaining legitimate access. Small delays or additional steps before AI activation reduce impulsive usage and promote mindful decision-making (Lyngs et al., 2019). Progressive AI reduction protocols, similar to addiction treatment, effectively reduce dependency, allowing individuals to rebuild cognitive capabilities without anxiety or performance decrements (Bhargava & Velasquez, 2021).

Metacognitive Awareness and Intentional AI Use

Developing metacognitive awareness—understanding one's cognitive processes and AI usage patterns—is crucial for maintaining autonomy. Metacognitive awareness improves self-regulation and decision-making in technology use (Efklides, 2008). The "intention-behavior gap" explains overuse; implementation intentions (specific if-then plans) improve alignment between intended and actual AI usage (Sheeran & Webb, 2016).

Cognitive load theory guides optimal human-AI task allocation, where humans handle tasks matching their capacity and delegate routine tasks to AI, preventing both cognitive overload and underutilization (Sweller et al., 2019). "AI literacy"—understanding how AI systems work, their limitations, and appropriate uses—improves human-AI collaboration and decision-making, reducing susceptibility to automation bias (Long & Magerko, 2020). Regular self-monitoring of cognitive performance provides feedback for adjusting

AI usage, helping individuals decide when to seek external assistance (Dunlosky & Metcalfe, 2009).

Physical Exercise and Neuroplasticity Enhancement

Physical exercise is a powerful intervention for cognitive health. Aerobic exercise promotes neuroplasticity and cognitive function through increased BDNF production, enhanced neurogenesis, and improved vascular health (Voss et al., 2013). Aerobic exercise training increases hippocampal volume and improves memory, counteracting technology-related hippocampal atrophy (Erickson et al., 2011).

The cognitive benefits of exercise are particularly pronounced for executive function, working memory, and attention—the domains most affected by AI over-reliance. High-intensity interval training (HIIT) improves cognitive flexibility and reduces mind-wandering (Heisz et al., 2017). Resistance training also contributes to cognitive health, improving executive function and reducing brain atrophy (Liu-Ambrose et al., 2010). The combination of aerobic and resistance training provides synergistic cognitive benefits (Colcombe & Kramer, 2003).

The timing of exercise relative to AI use affects cognitive outcomes; exercise immediately before cognitively demanding tasks improves performance and reduces the need for external cognitive aids (Pontifex et al., 2019).

FRAMEWORKS FOR BENEFICIAL HUMAN-AI COLLABORATION

The Complementary Intelligence Model

The complementary intelligence model emphasizes the unique strengths of both human and artificial intelligence, rather than viewing AI as a replacement for human cognition. Humans excel in creativity, empathy, and complex reasoning, while AI excels in pattern recognition, data processing, and consistent execution (Wilson & Daugherty, 2018).

"Human-in-the-loop" design ensures human decision-making authority while leveraging AI for data processing and preliminary analysis. Systems with meaningful human oversight produce better outcomes and maintain human cognitive engagement (Amershi et al., 2019). Cognitive amplification, rather than replacement, is the optimal framework, where AI systems extend rather than substitute human capabilities (Engelbart, 1962; Clark & Chalmers, 1998).

"Cognitive apprenticeship" with AI systems allows humans to learn from AI processes while maintaining their own cognitive skills (Collins et al., 1989; Hollan et al., 2000). Task rotation between human and AI execution maintains cognitive skills while benefiting from AI efficiency, preventing skill degradation associated with continuous automation (Parasuraman et al., 2000).

Adaptive Automation and Dynamic Task Allocation

Adaptive automation systems adjust their assistance based on human cognitive state and task demands, maintaining human engagement while providing support. Adaptive automation can maintain human skills while improving overall system performance (Kaber & Riley, 1999). Physiological monitoring technologies can assess cognitive load to trigger automated assistance only when humans are experiencing overload, preserving engagement during normal functioning (Gevins & Smith, 2003).

The increasing integration of Artificial Intelligence (AI) into human cognitive functions presents both significant opportunities and challenges for cognitive health. This analysis of scientific literature clearly indicates that over-reliance on AI can lead to measurable alterations in brain structure and function, impacting attention, memory, critical thinking, and decision-making autonomy.

These changes are rooted in neurobiological mechanisms. The brain's use-dependent plasticity dictates that unexercised cognitive functions weaken, while neural pathways supporting AI-mediated behaviors strengthen. This can result in cognitive atrophy, extending beyond simple skill loss to fundamental shifts in human information processing and decision-making.

However, these effects are not inevitable. Research shows that evidence-based interventions such as cognitive training, structured AI abstinence, physical exercise, and metacognitive awareness can effectively counteract negative impacts while preserving the benefits of human-AI collaboration. The goal is not to avoid AI, but to develop sophisticated interaction approaches that maintain human cognitive autonomy while leveraging AI capabilities.

The complementary intelligence model provides a framework for beneficial human-AI collaboration. AI systems perform best when they augment human capabilities in areas where AI excels, while preserving human involvement in domains requiring creativity, empathy, and complex reasoning. This necessitates thoughtful system design, user education, and continuous monitoring to ensure optimal outcomes.

Implementing these principles requires a coordinated effort. Individuals must develop personal strategies for managing AI interaction and maintaining cognitive health. Educational institutions should integrate AI literacy and cognitive wellness into curricula. Organizations must implement policies that promote beneficial human-AI collaboration and prevent over-reliance. Researchers must continue to investigate optimal interaction patterns and develop evidence-based interventions.

The stakes in optimizing human-AI interaction are considerable. Cognitive capabilities essential to human value—creativity, empathy, critical thinking, and complex reasoning—require active cultivation and protection in an AI-saturated environment. The objective is not to compete with AI, but to maintain the cognitive capacities that enable humans to direct, evaluate, and benefit from AI. As AI systems become more sophisticated and ubiquitous, safeguarding human cognitive autonomy will become increasingly vital.

This essay lays a foundation for beneficial human-AI collaboration, but ongoing research and adaptation are crucial as technology evolves. The future of human cognitive health in an AI world depends on our collective commitment to evidence-based approaches that preserve human agency while embracing technological capability. The path forward involves recognizing human and artificial intelligence as collaborators, not competitors, in solving complex challenges that neither could address alone. By maintaining human cognitive health while leveraging AI, we can create a future where technology amplifies, rather than replaces, human potential.

REFERENCES

- Acar, S., Burnett, C., & Cabra, J. F. (2017). Ingredients of creativity: Originality and more. *Creativity Research Journal*, 29(2), 133-144.
- Amershi, S., Cakmak, M., Knox, W. B., & Kulesza, T. (2014). Power to the people: The role of humans in interactive machine learning. *AI Magazine*, 35(4), 105-120.
- Amershi, S., Weld, D., Vorvoreanu, M., Fourney, A., Nushi, B., Collisson, P., ... & Horvitz, E. (2019). Guidelines for human-AI interaction. *Proceedings of the 2019 CHI Conference on Human Factors in Computing Systems*, 1-13.

- Au, J., Sheehan, E., Tsai, N., Duncan, G. J., Buschkuehl, M., & Jaeggi, S. M. (2015). Improving fluid intelligence with training on working memory: a meta-analysis. *Psychonomic Bulletin & Review*, 22(2), 366-377.
- Barr, N., Pennycook, G., Stolz, J. A., & Fugelsang, J. A. (2015). The brain in your pocket: Evidence that smartphones are used to supplant thinking. *Computers in Human Behavior*, 48, 473-480.
- Bhargava, A., & Velasquez, M. (2021). Ethics of the attention economy: The problem of social media addiction. *Business Ethics Quarterly*, 31(3), 321-359.
- Bohbot, V. D., Lerch, J., Thorndycraft, B., Iaria, G., & Zijdenbos, A. P. (2017). Gray matter differences correlate with spontaneous strategies in a human virtual navigation task. *Journal of Neuroscience*, 27(38), 10078-10083.
- Brailovskaia, J., Schillack, H., & Margraf, J. (2020). Tell me why are you using social media (SM)! Relationship between reasons

for use of SM, SM flow, daily stress, depression, anxiety, and addictive SM use? An exploratory investigation of young adults in Germany. *Computers in Human Behavior*, 113, 106511.

- Carr, N. (2010). *The shallows: What the Internet is doing to our brains*. W. W. Norton & Company.
- Chang, A. M., Aeschbach, D., Duffy, J. F., & Czeisler, C. A. (2015). Evening use of light-emitting eReaders negatively affects sleep, circadian timing, and next-morning alertness. *Proceedings of the National Academy of Sciences*, 112(4), 1232-1237.
- Clark, A., & Chalmers, D. (1998). The extended mind. *Analysis*, 58(1), 7-19.
- Clayton, R. B., Leshner, G., & Almond, A. (2011). The extended iSelf: The impact of iPhone separation on cognition, emotion, and physiology. *Journal of Computer-Mediated Communication*, 20(2), 119-135.
- Colcombe, S., & Kramer, A. F. (2003). Fitness effects on the cognitive function of

older adults: a meta-analytic study. *Psychological Science*, 14(2), 125-130.

- Collins, A., Brown, J. S., & Holum, A. (1991). Cognitive apprenticeship: Making thinking visible. *American Educator*, 15(3), 6-11.
- Diamond, A. (2013). Executive functions. *Annual Review of Psychology*, 64, 135-168.
- Dunlosky, J., & Metcalfe, J. (2009). *Metacognition*. Sage Publications.
- Efklides, A. (2008). Metacognition: Defining its facets and levels of functioning in relation to self-regulation and co-regulation. *European Psychologist*, 13(4), 277-287.
- Engelbart, D. C. (1962). Augmenting human intellect: A conceptual framework. Stanford Research Institute.
- Endsley, M. R., & Kaber, D. B. (1999). Level of automation effects on performance, situation awareness and workload in a dynamic control task. *Ergonomics*, 42(3), 462-492.

- Ericsson, A., & Pool, R. (2016). *Peak: Secrets from the new science of expertise.* Houghton Mifflin Harcourt.
- Erickson, K. I., Voss, M. W., Prakash, R. S., Basak, C., Szabo, A., Chaddock, L., ... & Kramer, A. F. (2011). Exercise training increases size of hippocampus and improves memory. *Proceedings of the National Academy of Sciences*, 108(7), 3017-3022.
- Gevins, A., & Smith, M. E. (2003). Neurophysiological measures of cognitive workload during human-computer interaction. *Theoretical Issues in Ergonomics Science*, 4(1-2), 113-131.
- Goddard, K., Roudsari, A., & Wyatt, J. C. (2012). Automation bias: a systematic review of frequency, effect mediators, and mitigators. *Journal of the American Medical Informatics Association*, 19(1), 121-127.
- Gradisar, M., Wolfson, A. R., Harvey, A. G., Hale, L., Rosenberg, R., & Czeisler, C. A. (2013). The sleep and technology use of Americans: findings from the National Sleep Foundation's 2011 Sleep in America

poll. *Journal of Clinical Sleep Medicine*, 9(12), 1291-1299.

- Grover, S., & Pea, R. (2013). Computational thinking in K-12: A review of the state of the field. *Educational Researcher*, 42(1), 38-43.
- Heisz, J. J., Clark, I. B., Bonin, K., Paolucci, E. M., Michalski, B., Becker, S., & Fahnestock, M. (2017). The effects of physical exercise and cognitive training on memory and neurotrophic factors. *Journal of Cognitive Neuroscience*, 29(11), 1895-1907.
- Hollan, J., Hutchins, E., & Kirsh, D. (2000). Distributed cognition: toward a new foundation for human-computer interaction research. *ACM Transactions on Computer-Human Interaction*, 7(2), 174-196.
- Hölzel, B. K., Carmody, J., Vangel, M., Congleton, C., Yerramsetti, S. M., Gard, T., & Lazar, S. W. (2011). Mindfulness practice leads to increases in regional brain gray matter density. *Psychiatry Research: Neuroimaging*, 191(1), 36-43.

- Horvitz, E. (1999). Principles of mixed-initiative user interfaces. *Proceedings of the SIGCHI Conference on Human Factors in Computing Systems*, 159-166.
- Jaeggi, S. M., Buschkuehl, M., Jonides, J., & Perrig, W. J. (2008). Improving fluid intelligence with training on working memory. *Proceedings of the National Academy of Sciences*, 105(19), 6829-6833.
- Jameson, A. (2003). Adaptive interfaces and agents. *Human-Computer Interaction: Design Issues, Solutions, and Applications*, 105-130.
- Kaber, D. B., & Riley, J. M. (1999). Adaptive automation of a dynamic control task based on secondary task workload measurement. *The International Journal of Cognitive Ergonomics*, 3(3), 169-187.
- Kahneman, D., & Frederick, S. (2002). Representativeness revisited: Attribute substitution in intuitive judgment. *Heuristics and Biases: The Psychology of Intuitive Judgment*, 49-81.

- Kaplan, S. (1995). The restorative benefits of nature: Toward an integrative framework. *Journal of Environmental Psychology*, 15(3), 169-182.
- Karanam, Y., Filko, L., Kaser, E., Alotaibi, H., Voona, S. R., & Plass, J. L. (2020). Supporting cognitive offloading in technology-enhanced learning environments. *Educational Technology Research and Development*, 68(2), 639-662.
- Kelly, A. C., & Garavan, H. (2005). Human functional neuroimaging of brain changes associated with practice. *Cerebral Cortex*, 15(8), 1089-1102.
- Klein, G., Woods, D. D., Bradshaw, J. M., Hoffman, R. R., & Feltovich, P. J. (2004). Ten challenges for making automation a "team player" in joint human-agent activity. *IEEE Intelligent Systems*, 19(6), 91-95.
- Levenson, J. C., Shensa, A., Sidani, J. E., Colditz, J. B., & Primack, B. A. (2016). The association between social media use and

sleep disturbance among young adults. *Preventive Medicine*, 85, 36-41.

- Leroy, S. (2009). Why is it so hard to do my work? The challenge of attention residue when switching between work tasks. *Organizational Behavior and Human Decision Processes*, 109(2), 168-181.
- Liu-Ambrose, T., Nagamatsu, L. S., Graf, P., Beattie, B. L., Ashe, M. C., & Handy, T. C. (2010). Resistance training and executive functions: a 12-month randomized controlled trial. *Archives of Internal Medicine*, 170(2), 170-178.
- Loh, K. K., & Kanai, R. (2016). How has the Internet reshaped human cognition? *The Neuroscientist*, 22(5), 506-520.
- Long, D., & Magerko, B. (2020). What is AI literacy? Competencies and design considerations. *Proceedings of the 2020 CHI Conference on Human Factors in Computing Systems*, 1-16.
- Lyngs, U., Lukoff, K., Slovak, P., Binns, R., Slack, A., Inzlicht, M., ... & Shadbolt, N. (2019). Self-control in cyberspace: Ap-

plying dual systems theory to a review of digital self-control tools. *Proceedings of the 2019 CHI Conference on Human Factors in Computing Systems*, 1-18.

- Maier, S. F., & Seligman, M. E. (2016). Learned helplessness at fifty: Insights from neuroscience. *Psychological Review*, 123(4), 349-367.
- Mark, G., Gudith, D., & Klocke, U. (2008). The cost of interrupted work: more speed and stress. *Proceedings of the SIGCHI Conference on Human Factors in Computing Systems*, 107-110.
- Merzenich, M. M., Van Vleet, T. M., & Nahum, M. (2014). Brain plasticity-based therapeutics. *Frontiers in Human Neuroscience*, 8, 385.
- Mueller, P. A., & Oppenheimer, D. M. (2014). The pen is mightier than the keyboard: Advantages of longhand over laptop note taking. *Psychological Science*, 25(6), 1159-1168.
- Ophir, E., Nass, C., & Wagner, A. D. (2009). Cognitive control in media multi-

taskers. *Proceedings of the National Academy of Sciences*, 106(37), 15583-15587.

- Parasuraman, R., & Riley, V. (1997). Humans and automation: Use, misuse, disuse, abuse. *Human Factors*, 39(2), 230-253.
- Parasuraman, R., Sheridan, T. B., & Wickens, C. D. (2000). A model for types and levels of human interaction with automation. *IEEE Transactions on Systems, Man, and Cybernetics-Part A: Systems and Humans*, 30(3), 286-297.
- Parker, S. K., Morgeson, F. P., & Johns, G. (2017). One hundred years of work design research: Looking back and looking forward. *Journal of Applied Psychology*, 102(3), 403-420.
- Pontifex, M. B., McGowan, A. L., Chandler, M. C., Gwizdala, K. L., Parks, A. C., Fenn, K., & Kamijo, K. (2019). A primer on investigating the after effects of acute bouts of physical activity on cognition. *Psychology of Sport and Exercise*, 40, 1-22.
- Posner, M. I., & Petersen, S. E. (1990). The attention system of the human brain.

Annual Review of Neuroscience, 13(1), 25-42.

- Primack, B. A., Shensa, A., Sidani, J. E., Whaite, E. O., yi Lin, L., Rosen, D., ... & Miller, E. (2017). Social media use and perceived social isolation among young adults in the US. *American Journal of Preventive Medicine*, 53(1), 1-8.
- Radesky, J. S., Schumacher, J., & Zuckerman, B. (2015). Mobile and interactive media use by young children: the good, the bad, and the unknown. *Pediatrics*, 135(1), 1-3.
- Ramos, C., Augusto, J. C., & Shapiro, D. (2008). Ambient intelligence—the next step for artificial intelligence. *IEEE Intelligent Systems*, 23(2), 15-18.
- Ribeiro, M. T., Singh, S., & Guestrin, C. (2016). "Why should I trust you?" Explaining the predictions of any classifier. *Proceedings of the 22nd ACM SIGKDD International Conference on Knowledge Discovery and Data Mining*, 1135-1144.
- Rosen, L. D., Whaling, K., Rab, S., Carrier, L. M., & Cheever, N. A. (2013). Is Face-

book creating "iDisorders"? The link between clinical symptoms of psychiatric disorders and technology use, attitudes and anxiety. *Computers in Human Behavior*, 29(3), 1243-1254.

- Rosen, L. D., Lim, A. F., Felt, J., Carrier, L. M., Cheever, N. A., Lara-Ruiz, J. M., ... & Rokkum, J. (2014). Media and technology use predicts ill-being among children, preteens and teenagers independent of the negative health impacts of exercise and eating habits. *Computers in Human Behavior*, 35, 364-375.
- Schultz, W. (2015). Neuronal reward and decision signals: from theories to data. *Physiological Reviews*, 95(3), 853-951.
- Schraw, G., & Dennison, R. S. (1994). Assessing metacognitive awareness. *Contemporary Educational Psychology*, 19(4), 460-475.
- Seligman, M. E. (1972). Learned helplessness: Problems, perspective, and program. *American Psychologist*, 27(5), 407-412.

- Sheeran, P., & Webb, T. L. (2016). The intention-behavior gap. *Social and Personality Psychology Compass*, 10(9), 503-518.
- Sparrow, B., Liu, J., & Wegner, D. M. (2011). Google effects on memory: Cognitive consequences of having information at our fingertips. *Science*, 333(6043), 776-778.
- Stone, L. (2006). Continuous partial attention. *Linda Stone*. Retrieved from https://lindastone.net/qa/continuous-partial-attention/
- Sunstein, C. R. (2019). *How change happens*. MIT Press.
- Sweller, J., van Merriënboer, J. J., & Paas, F. (2019). Cognitive architecture and instructional design: 20 years later. *Educational Psychology Review*, 31(2), 261-292.
- Thomée, S., Härenstam, A., & Hagberg, M. (2011). Mobile phone use and stress, sleep disturbances, and symptoms of depression among young adults-a prospective cohort study. *BMC Public Health*, 11(1), 66.
- Turel, O., He, Q., Xue, G., Xiao, L., & Bechara, A. (2014). Examination of neural

systems sub-serving Facebook "addiction". *Psychological Reports*, 115(3), 675-695.

- Turkle, S. (2011). *Alone together: Why we expect more from technology and less from each other*. Basic Books.
- Voss, M. W., Vivar, C., Kramer, A. F., & van Praag, H. (2013). The influence of aerobic fitness on cerebral white matter integrity and cognitive function in older adults. *Human Brain Mapping*, 34(11), 2972-2985.
- Ward, A. F., Duke, K., Gneezy, A., & Bos, M. W. (2017). Brain drain: The mere presence of one's own smartphone reduces available cognitive capacity. *Journal of the Association for Consumer Research*, 2(2), 140-154.
- Wilson, H. J., & Daugherty, P. R. (2018). Collaborative intelligence: Humans and AI are joining forces. *Harvard Business Review*, 96(4), 114-123.
- Wing, J. M. (2006). Computational thinking. *Communications of the ACM*, 49(3), 33-35.

- Wood, D., Bruner, J. S., & Ross, G. (1976). The role of tutoring in problem solving. *Journal of Child Psychology and Psychiatry*, 17(2), 89-100.
- Zeidan, F., Johnson, S. K., Diamond, B. J., David, Z., & Goolkasian, P. (2010). Mindfulness meditation improves cognition: evidence of brief mental training. *Consciousness and Cognition*, 19(2), 597-605.

www.ingramcontent.com/pod-product-compliance
Lightning Source LLC
LaVergne TN
LVHW022030200926
848481LV00007B/2618
* 9 7 9 8 3 4 9 6 8 4 1 2 8 *